T0031198

THE LITTLE BOOK OF
ABUELITA
WISDOM

FOR WHEN YOU NEED A
BIT OF GUIDANCE FROM ABUELA

RAVEN ISHAK

ILLUSTRATED BY
JOSEFINA SCHARGORODSKY

RUNNING PRESS
PHILADELPHIA

Running Press
Hachette Book Group
1290 Avenue of the Americas, New York, NY 10104
www.runningpress.com
@Running_Press

Printed in China

First Edition: April 2024

Published by Running Press, an imprint of Hachette Book Group, Inc.
The Running Press name and logo are trademarks of Hachette Book Group, Inc.

The Hachette Speakers Bureau provides a wide range of authors for
speaking events. To find out more, go to www.hachettespeakersbureau.com
or email HachetteSpeakers@hbgusa.com.

Running Press books may be purchased in bulk for business, educational,
or promotional use. For more information, please contact your local
bookseller or the Hachette Book Group Special Markets Department at
Special.Markets@hbgusa.com.

The publisher is not responsible for websites (or their content) that are
not owned by the publisher.

Print book cover and interior design by Amanda Richmond

LCCN: 2023013603

ISBNs: 978-0-7624-8420-1 (hardcover); 978-0-7624-8422-5 (ebook)

APS

10   9   8   7   6   5   4   3   2   1

CONTENTS

A LETTER FROM ABUELA . . . 5

If you need help cleaning tu casa,
go to page 11

**If you need a reminder on
how to be confident,**
go to page 27

**If you're sick
and need help feeling better,**
go to page 34

If you need money and career tips,
go to page 49

If you miss abuela's cooking,
go to page 59

**If you are going to
celebrate the holidays,**
go to page 67

**If you need help with
your relationship,**
go to page 81

**If you need help with maintaining
the spark with your spouse,**
go to page 99

**If you are going through
a hard time,**
go to page 113

A GOODBYE LETTER
FROM ABUELA . . . 127

A LETTER FROM ABUELA

Mi corazón, the apple of my
eye, my golden grandchild
(por favor don't tell your primos,
pero you know this to be true . . .),

As your abuela, I feel that I have the responsibility to show you the meaning of life. As the matriarch of this familia, I have the duty to tell you the difference between right and wrong. But as tu amiga, tu confidant y tu partner in crime, I have the obligation to shower you with amor, grace, support, and protection, and to show you how to have fun—after all, life shouldn't be taken so seriously (which your tía is still learning . . . ay, mi preciosa).

When tu mamá gave birth to you, I knew that you were going to bring so much happiness and joy into this world. When you were a little bebé and I held you in my arms and looked into your eyes, I knew that you were going to be the love of my life. I asked myself, *How could someone just entering this world be so pure and full of light?* And that's when I knew God was always going to watch over you, just like me, tu abuela.

Ever since that moment, I climbed mountains and crawled through the trenches to look after you and to make sure you were going to be okay. Sí, tienes el amor de tu mamá, pero there is nothing like having an abuela. We cook for the whole familia, we invite people over to play dominoes and drink café con leches (we do know how to throw a good party), and we teach our grandchildren how to grow up and become respectful, confident, and thoughtful adults. To me, there is nothing like an abuela's love. (Call me biased, pero it's true.)

I know that our relationship wasn't always perfect, mi amor. After all, we grew up in different times, and I know that I can have strong opinions about certain things. But that doesn't mean I love you less—if anything, it makes me love you mucho, mucho más (even though you give me a dolor de cabeza sometimes). Just know that my love for you isn't conditional, mi amor. My love is endless, infinite, boundless—and even when I am not here, I will love you, now and forever. And I don't want you to forget that.

So, after everything that we have been through, I want you to know, mi amor, that I will always be there for you no matter what—just like how you've been there for me (abuela is strong, pero sometimes she needs tender loving care too). And that's why it means the world to me that you are seeking my advice. I know you could go to your little friends, and I know that you could even ask your partner (if you have one, pero don't worry if you don't—they will come); however, you coming to abuela for help makes me feel so loved.

¡Ay, okay! Enough of the mushy-mushy, mi amor. Don't worry, I am going to tell you everything that I know about life, love, cooking, confidence, and more. As my grandchild, you should never go through life alone—so I am going to tell you everything you need to know, even if it's sometimes hard to hear.

Do you want to know how to cook abuela's famous dishes? I'll give you some of my best recipes. ¡Tienes que comer para ser fuerte!

Do you want to know how to find a good partner like how I found tu abuelo? (Because, believe it or not, your abuela was a sexy woman. ¡Todavía lo soy, caramba!) I will tell you what a healthy and respectful relationship should look like.

Do you want to know how to get through hard times? I'll give you advice about failure, breakups, and everything in between.

This little book of my wisdom will guide you through every chapter of your life—and I hope it provides you the peace you are looking for (pero remember, mi amor, you can always ask God for guidance too). And as time goes on, I want you to revisit these pages to remember me and the love that I have for you porque it is not going anywhere.

Te quiero mucho, siempre,
Tu abuela

MAKING A HOUSE FEEL LIKE A HOME

Quiero que escuches
atentamente, mi corazón...

I know you want to "hang" con tus amiguitos or do a little "self-care" routine (as the kids call it these days)—and know that I say this with love—pero tu casa is not a piggy pen and it needs to be cleaned every weekend. Punto. Then afterward you can hang out with your little friends. ¿Okay? *Porque como tienes tu espacio, así tienes la mente.*

When I was your age, I would have the house cleaned from top to bottom. Do you ever remember coming to my house and it looking like a garbage dump? I don't think so. ¡Podrías comer del suelo if you wanted to! Ay, pero don't do that; you are not a little piggy. Also, have you eaten yet?—Te ves todo hueso. Te voy a hacer algo de comida. Mira, now you are distracting me!

Either way, I don't want you to worry, mi cielo. I'm going to tell you everything you need to know when it comes to cleaning so you will have a spotless home. *Escoba que no se gasta, casa que no se limpia.*

THE LITTLE BOOK OF ABUELITA WISDOM

Abuela's Guiding Principles of Cleaning

∽

Mira, as much as I want to share with you every little tip on how to clean every little thing in your home, I don't have the time because I need to watch my novelas and you are an adult (even though you will always be my little angel in my eyes), and sometimes you need to figure out your own rhythm when it comes to creating your own home. However, there are a few "guidelines" you can follow that are abuela-approved, so por favor, escúchame:

1. Clean while you cook. Siempre.
2. Make tu cama in the mañana.
3. Always have nice-smelling candles burning.
4. Para nietas: you never want to clean a man's dirty underwear. Punto.
5. Do not ever throw away perfectly good bolsas, food containers, or socks. They can be repurposed for other things, mi amor.

If you follow these five steps then everything else will fall into place, mi amor.

CLEANING SUPPLIES YOU'LL NEED

- Fabuloso
- harapos (rags)
- trapeador (mop)
- Celia Cruz, Gloria Estefan, and Joe Arroyo (para música)
- newspaper
- baking soda y vinegar
- cinnamon sticks

Step 1: Wake up early on sábado y ponte un café en la estufa. *¡Ponte las pilas! Al que madruga, Dios le ayuda.* Believe me, you will need a Café Bustelo to move that culito. (Digo esto con amor.)

Step 2: Put your phone away and play one of your records, like Celia Cruz, Elvis Crespo, and Joe Arroyo. Don't bring that Bad Bunny or Daddy Yankee into your home. Nada de ese taki taki. Remember God is watching. Okay, I do like some of their songs, pero don't tell your mother.

💜 ABUELA TIP 💜

When you put your teléfono away, you won't be distracted by those "ticktacs" or Facebook text messages. Confía en mí, mi amor. However, if you want to call abuela every once in a while, I can keep you company when you're cleaning. Just putting it out there, mi amor.

Step 3: Open all the windows and curtains in your home. You have to let the light in so you can see all the dust and dirt on the floor. This will also bring fresh air into your home and let out all the malas vibras. If not, one of your tías will tell you exactly where you missed a spot the next time she comes over to visit. (Also, have you called your tía? You should; she's been asking about you.)

💜 ABUELA TIP 💜

You can also use this time to clean your windows and mirrors. Make a mixture of equal parts vinegar and water. Spray it onto a piece of newspaper and wipe the surface until both windows and mirrors are sparkling and smudge-free, just like your beautiful smile. The newspaper works better porque it has a gritty texture to act as a light polisher, and it's more absorbent because of its denser fiber. See, abuela knows her little tricks.

Step 4: Next, you want to go into each room and spray Fabuloso (o un baking soda y vinegar mixture) y clean every surface con tu trapo or trapeador— and don't be lazy with this, mija, mijo. Again, God is watching and will know. You have to move every single item that you have on your dressers, counters, and pisos. Maybe if you got rid of some of the things you don't need, you could have fewer things to clean. I know you don't like to hear this, mi amor, pero just think about it.

💗 **ABUELA TIP** 💗

Mi amor, if you can, try to only have things that are most important to you and get rid of the rest. Remember: it's more important to take care of the things you currently have than buying the latest "trendy" thing. You can also use that extra money to buy something nice para tu mamá o papá—pero it's just my two cents.

Whether you are cleaning tu dormitorio o tu baño, remember to clean de arriba a abajo. You don't clean the floors without wiping the counters first. You don't vacuum without dusting the shelves first. ¿Tú entiendes, mi amor? When you clean tu casa like this, you won't have to go back to clean again if any dust or crumbs fall on the piso. You have to do it right the first time—and that is a lesson in life, mi corazón.

Step 5: After you clean your entire home, put a pot on the stove con agua and cinnamon sticks. Let it boil so the smell of cinnamon cleans the air. This will get rid of any stinky smells that may still be lingering in your home. Don't be ashamed, mi amor. Our homes get smelly every once in a while—pero if you stay on top of your cleaning, you won't feel as embarrassed. Don't worry, abuela loves you no matter what.

You can also do this after cooking heavy meals that smell strong like fish or oil, mija, mijo. Pero you wouldn't have to worry about this too much if you clean after you cook like I taught you when you were little. *No es más limpio quien más limpia, sino quien menos ensucia.*

And that's it, mi vida. Your house is ready for visitors. Don't forget to put las flores en un florero. (My favorite are carnations. Está bien si lo olvidaste, mi corazón, te amo.) Pero if your tías come over, just ignore their comments about your home. (Ellas siempre están hablando tonterías.)

Ay, and don't let tus primos pequeños make a mess in tu casa. I had to stop all of you from making a mess in my home when all of you were little, especially when you all didn't like what I made for breakfast. (I have to lie down . . . I am getting a headache just thinking about it.)

Abuela's Spring
Cleaning Must-Dos

∾

Okay, even though you should be doing this every time you clean, I know you don't have a lot of time on your hands between hanging out with your friends and going to work (or la escuela), so when springtime comes, please deep clean tu casa with these little tips:

• **Declutter everything in your home.** Ay . . . do you really need twenty pairs of shoes or hundreds of books that you could just borrow from the library? Get rid of some things, por favor. Donate it to people in need.

💜 **ABUELA PRONUNCIATION** 💜

Se dice "choos" no shoes.

• **Clean your baseboards, behind big appliances, light fixtures, cupboards, walls, and your shower head.** I recommend soaking the shower head with vinegar, pero a normal cleaner will do just fine. And use regular soap and water for everything else. Your house will not become a home if you have dirty fixtures or walls, mi amor.

 • **Put saints all around your house to protect your home.** Since abuela can't always be there to protect you, please let God watch over you. Do this for me, por favor. Que Dios te bendiga siempre.

• **Use bleach when necessary.** Sí, Dawn y Fabuloso are perfecto for cleaning, pero nothing works as well as bleach. Just be careful not to breathe in the fumes, mi corazón. And use gloves and an apron to protect yourself. I don't want to receive a call from tu mama because you didn't listen to abuela.

HOW TO FOLD A FITTED SHEET

Ay, if there is one thing I want you to remember how to do for the rest of your life (besides calling your abuela, of course), it is to know how to fold a fitted sheet. My mother taught me how to do this, and now I will teach you. It's simple once you know—and then you can teach your spouse and your future children. (You are planning to have kids, right? I'm not getting any younger.)

Step 1: Hold the sheet lengthwise with the opening of the sheet facing you.

Step 2: Put las manos in the top two corners of the sheet and hold them up, like you are praying.

Step 3: Bring the two corners together by folding one end over the other end, so they are now on top of one another on one of your hands.

Step 4: Have your other hand straighten the edge of the sheet as you reach for the other corner of the sheet to keep everything together.

Step 5: Once you have your hand in the opposite corner, you should now have both manos in each corner again like before.

Step 6: You will repeat step 3 again by folding one corner over the other, so they are now on top of one another. Are you following, mi amor? Put the phone down!

Step 7: Take your other hand to straighten the edge of the sheet and lay it on the ground so the opening of the sheet is still facing you.

Step 8: Fold one part of the sheet so it looks like a long rectangle. This will make folding the entire sheet much easier, mi amor.

Step 9: Finally, fold the sheet again lengthwise and then fold the sheet horizontally two more times.

Now you know how to fold a fitted sheet correctly, into a nice little square!

HOW TO DECORATE
YOUR HOME LIKE ABUELA

¡Okay! Now that tu casa is clean from top to bottom, it's time to make your house feel like a home—and who better to ask than your abuela! I'm so glad you came to me, I've been meaning to talk to you about how you decorated your home. It's nice, pero it's time for it to look like a grown-up lives there, porque how are you going to find a partner if you are still sleeping on cartoon sheets?

DECORATIONS TO
HAVE IN YOUR HOME

• **Plenty of decorative pillows for your bed and a nice duvet or comforter.** Do you want your bed to look put together? Then you'll need to buy some decorative pillows and a duvet or comforter. No, you won't actually sleep with these pillows, pero that's not the point; they are there to show guests that you know how to make a proper bed. Punto.

• **Hang decorative hand towels in your bathroom.** Ay, don't roll your eyes at me, mi corazón. A well-put-together bathroom means having matching hand towels, a toilet seat cover, a little decorative angel by the sink, a small light outlet that lights the bathroom in the dark so you can see, a basket full of magazines for guests to enjoy while they do their business, and a matching shower curtain and floormat.

• **Put placemats underneath your plates to protect the table linen.** ¿Qué? You don't have table linen for your dinner table? That's a sin. Por favor, buy a table cover to protect your mesa, *ahora*. Then you can find placemats to complement la mesa. Don't forget to place decorative flowers in the middle of the table too. It's okay if they are plastic—no one will know the difference.

• **A religious artifact to look over you.** Even if it's a small one by your desk, it's important to show appreciation and love for our faith.

• **A bowl of candies or chocolates for your guests to enjoy.** What are your guests going to snack on when they come over? Are you going to let them starve while they sit on the couch? If you want to be a good host, make sure to have multiple little containers or bowls filled with candies, chocolate, caramels, and so on around your home for guests to nibble on.

• **Add fun little magnets on your fridge to hold pictures of loved ones and important reminders.** A house won't feel like a home if the front and side of your fridge are empty, mi amor. Add little photos of tu familia and put little fruit, picture, or souvenir magnets to hold important papers and reminders like that doctor's appointment I hope you scheduled. (Do it for your health, mi amor.)

VALUING YOURSELF

From Beauty to Confidence and Everything in Between

nother lesson I hope you take from this little book is the importance of valuing yourself, mi vida. Unfortunately, a lot of people in today's world may only consider you to be "valuable" if you have a "good" desk job with a high-paying salary and a home—pero that is not true. Your abuelo didn't have any of those things, so does that make him less valuable? Tu mamá y papá didn't own a home until many years into their marriage, so does that mean they don't bring value to this society? Your value is there no matter who you are and what you do, mi amor. You don't need to prove anything to anyone to be considered importante.

Of course, I want you to have all of those things because it means you made it in America, pero being successful in America doesn't change where your family came from and how hard we fought to get here, and you should never push your history aside to try to "fit in," especially if other people are choosing not to accept you for who you are or where you came from. These people do not and will not ever define your worth— only you and God can do this. Not even me, mi corazón.

I wish I could tell you that the world will show up kindly to those who look and act like us, pero that is not always the case. The world can be tough and unforgiving; however, that doesn't mean you should cause the same pain back to them. ¿Por qué? It will not prove anything, and this is not the way Diosito wants us to live. Remember, mi amor: you are a child of God, and it is your job to show kindness everywhere you go. We do not judge, only God can do this.

I know this is easier said than done. When you're a child, you most likely won't feel discriminated against by those who choose to live with hate inside themselves, because you have abuela and your parent to protect you, pero as you get older, you may witness and be confronted with tough obstacles to overcome—and I wish with my whole being that I could shield you from this hurt and pain. However, just know that you have the strength within you to make the right choice—the best choice—for you. And just know that whatever choice you make won't devalue who you are.

Life is tough, mi cielo, but as long as you love who you are, respect who you are, and value who you are, then it doesn't matter what anyone else thinks.

Abuela's Definition of Beauty

When it comes to beauty and makeup, less is more. Punto. Your abuela likes to wear blue eyeshadow and lipstick every day, it's true, pero I need it more than you do! You have to remember that your beauty comes from within. Ay, but don't walk around looking like a bum, either. You never know who you might bump into (your boss, your doctor, a future partner who is also a doctor, uno nunca sabe). If you are going to wear makeup and do your hair, all you need are a few simple things.

ABUELA-APPROVED BEAUTY AND MAKEUP PRODUCTS

- Pond's moisturizer
- mascara
- Chanel N°5 perfume
- hot curlers
- baby powder
- bottles of lotion
- baby oil

Sí, these are things I use, pero what more do you need? I know you say you don't always need to look done up, mi sol, especially when you do errands, pero the last thing you want is to bump into the love of your life or a colleague looking like you just went through a garbage bin and miss an opportunity. ¡Oye! Don't tell me I'm being dramática. I heard this happened to your second cousin and he still talks about it. After all, you would never catch me going out in public without my hair done up to give my neighbors ammo for chisme. (But if they do talk about you, no les hagas caso, mi corazón.)

Either way, you shouldn't have to focus on your beauty too much ¡porque eres una hermosura! Sí, I know I am your abuela, and my eyes aren't what they used to be, pero it's true! I know when I see a good-looking person and that's you, mija, mijo! Besides, the apple doesn't fall too far from the tree—you came from your mother, who came from me, so, of course you are attractive! Pero if you want to feel more put together, it's important to always do these things every day to feel like your best self.

💕 ABUELA PRONUNCIATION 💕

Ay, I know the way I pronounce "focus" sometimes sounds like a bad word, pero your abuela has a dirty mouth sometimes—so it's okay.

ABUELA'S TOP RULES TO FEEL PUT TOGETHER

• **Wear clean underwear, *siempre*.** What happens if you get into an accident and the medical professionals have to shred your clothes because you injured yourself? Do you *want* them to see that you are walking around with dirty underwear? I don't think so, mi amor. In fact, always bring a clean pair of underwear with you wherever you go, just in case.

• **Clean the absolute most important parts of your body.** Escúchame, if you can't take a shower, por favor, clean the most important parts of your body: your private parts and your underarms. You don't want to go around smelling like trasero and people saying "fo" behind your back. Mira, I will love you no matter what, pero try to spend less time on your phone and more time cleaning your body, okay, mi amor? Your friends and partner will thank you.

• **Pray for what you're grateful for or do your rosaries every night.** Porque what is more important than praying to God? To have an appreciation for life, you must show appreciation to God.

💜 **ABUELA TIP** 💜

Ay, por favor, don't rush through doing your prayers like when you were little, okay? I may not be there to pray with you when you're older, pero God will know.

• **Stand up straight.** Why are you slouching, baby? You are too precious to sit at your desk or stand around with a hunch on your back. Do you want to grow old with a hunchback? Stick your chest out and stand up straight ahora. You cannot feel good about yourself if you do not know how to carry yourself.

Be confident. It doesn't matter what you wear, how you do your hair, or how you present yourself if you don't have confidence. Once you have confidence, mi corazón, you will begin to feel more comfortable being and loving yourself—porque at the end of the day, that's all that matters.

💜 ABUELA TIP 💜

Mira, mi amor—if someone talks behind your back? Who cares! They must think about you enough to want to talk about you with others. If they let you go or fire you from a job? Show them who's boss by walking out with style and getting an even better job. If your significant other breaks up with you? Wave goodbye and send them on their way. *A mal tiempo buena cara.* None of these bad situations will stop you in your tracks if you have the confidence to move on and look forward, mi amor. Remember that.

HOW TO TAKE CARE OF
YOURSELF IF YOU'RE SICK

¡Ay, mi corazón! Are you sick? ¿Tienes fiebre? ¿Estás tosiendo? ¡Dígame! Also, is this because you've been working too hard, mi amor? I told you to slow down—why don't you listen to me? ¿O estuviste sin medias en la casa, con el pelo mojado? You didn't put on a suéter . . . Dios mío!

Okay, don't worry, mi preciosa, precioso, abuela is here to take care of you. First of all, you'll need to have a few things in your medicine cabinet. Either order these things online from the marketplace or have a loved one buy them for you. Whatever you do, mi amor, do not leave tu cama porque you'll get sicker— and I can't let my bebé get sick. *La salud es la mejor riqueza.*

COLD REMEDIES FROM ABUELA

- Vicks VapoRub (Vivaporú)
- sopa de pollo (with fresh lime juice)
- saltine crackers
- Sprite y ginger ale (if you're nauseated)
- manta (blanket) y medias (socks)
- steam
- hot water with lemon/lime and honey, or hot water with onion, honey, and lime
- chamomile, peppermint, or ginger tea
- Have someone sing to you "Sana, sana, colita de rana"
- an egg
- Gatorade

I know this is a long list, mi vida, pero tu abuela is going to tell you exactly what to do with each of these items. Don't worry, mi amor, you're going to feel better soon.

How to Use Vicks VapoRub

If there is one item you need to have in tu casa at all times, it's Vicks VapoRub. ¿Por qué? Porque you'll use this for every ailmentyou can imagine. Have a cut on your arm? Ponte Vicks. Have a stuffy nose? Ponte Vicks. Have swollen eyes after crying from a breakup even though I told you that person wasn't good enough for mi ángel? Ponte Vicks.

All you have to do, mi amor, is take a little bit of Vicks and rub it on the ailment. Here are some ways you can do this:

- Rub Vicks on your chest if you have a stuffy nose.
- Rub Vicks on the bottom of your feet and put socks on to get rid of a cold.
- Rub Vicks on your forehead if you have a headache.

You get the picture, mi amor.

How to Make Sopa de Pollo

୧

The minute—and I mean the minute—you sneeze, have someone whip up this sopa para ti, amor. This is abuela's famous recipe; one spoonful of this will cure any disease or sickness. Trust me, mi amor. In any case, you should have all these ingredients in your pantry already.

....

1 to 2 pounds bone-in chicken

Adobo seasoning (para pollo)

1 chicken bouillon cube

2 tablespoons sofrito (premade is fine, mi amor)

A pinch of salt and pepper (you know I don't like a lot of sodium, but I know you do, mi amor, pero don't go crazy)

4 to 5 long carrots

3 to 5 white or yellow potatoes (not rustic or sweet)

2 ears of corn (pero make sure to chop into smaller pieces)

3 cloves of garlic

A handful of pasta (use angel hair or spaghetti pasta, pero no linguine)

1 lime wedge, for serving (optional)

Cilantro, for serving (optional)

½ avocado, cubed, for serving (optional)

....

Season your pollo with adobo and sear the pollo slightly in a large pot over medium-high heat to make the outside a little crispy, about 4 minutes on each side (pero not too much, mi amor, you don't want to overcook it).

Next, take out the pollo, fill the pot with water, increase the heat to high, and let it come to a boil.

Once the water boils, add the bouillon, sofrito, and salt and pepper to the water. Stir until the bouillon is completely dissolved.

Next, put the seared pollo into el agua, lower heat to medium, and let it cook the rest of the way, about 25 minutes (pero time might be different based on your stove).

While the pollo is cooking, chop up the carrots, potatoes, corn, and garlic, and place it into the water once the pollo is cooked. Cover the pot and let it simmer over medium heat for 30 to 40 minutes (or until you can put a fork through the potatoes).

Once the vegetables are cooked, you can add the pasta to the pot and let it cook for as long as it says on the box to make sure it is fully cooked.

And that's it, mi amor. If you want to add more salt and pepper, go ahead. I would also suggest adding a squeeze of lime and a few pieces of cilantro into tu sopa. (Also, it doesn't hurt to have a few pieces of avocado on the side too.)

How to Use Saltine Crackers, Sprite, y Ginger Ale for an Upset Stomach

This is pretty straightforward, mi cielo, pero eating and drinking these three things will make your stomachache go away. You just have to make sure you get these exact brands: Premium Original Saltine Crackers, Sprite, y Canada Dry ginger ale. Once you have them, just place them on your nightstand and snack on them whenever you need a little pick-me-up.

♥ ABUELA PRONUNCIATION ♥
Mira, it's pronounced "Esprai" yo no sé nada de Sprite.

How to Use Mantas (Blankets) y Medias (Socks)

Mi bebé, grab every blanket you have in your home and put it over your body if you have a cold or fever. It's very important that you sweat out this fever for it to go away properly. But before you cover yourself with blankets, make sure to find cozy socks and put them on your little footsies to keep them warm. (I like to use the ones from the hospital, pero you can probably use the ones I got you for Navidad.) Also, don't forget to put Vivaporú on the bottom of your feet first.

How to Use Steam to Get Rid of a Stuffy Nose or Cold

Ay, mi amor. I am so sorry you're feeling sick. If the Vicks isn't working, then ponte agua en a pot and let it come to a boil. Once it boils, turn off the stove and pour the hot water into a heat-safe bowl, so you can breathe in the steam. Just make sure to cover your head with a small towel, so you can breathe most of that steam in. Be careful, mija, mijo. Don't put this bowl on a wobbly table or tu cama. You don't want to burn yourself. Remember abuela knows best.

How to Make Chamomile, Peppermint, or Ginger Tea

Ay, you have a good head on your shoulders, mi corazón. Let's put it to use here. (However, I do recommend using real ginger for the ginger tea. Just buy a ginger root, cut it up, and let it boil in hot water until it begins to look like tea—sip and enjoy!)

How to Make Hot Water with Limón and Honey o Red Onion and Honey Cough Syrup

Heat up about a cup of water over the stove, pour it into a cup, and then squeeze a few limones into the cup. Then put a spoonful of honey and stir it in the cup until it melts.

💜 ABUELA TIP 💜

The trick is to sip it while it's hot, mija, mijo. Don't watch your little programas and forget this drink exists! Pero if you don't have time to sip (you need to slow down, mi amor; you're working too much!), just take a spoonful of honey with a squeeze of limón on top—this will do the trick.

Red Onion and Honey Cough Syrup

∾

I know this sounds a little yucky, mi amor, pero trust me, it works. It's good for your immune system porque it will make it strong. This recipe is easy.

---

1 whole red onion
1 or 1½ cups honey

Thinly slice the red onion and place the slices in a medium bowl.

Pour the honey over the onion slices. You want to make sure you completely cover them, mi amor.

Let this mixture sit in the bowl for 2 to 3 hours. The mixture will make a syrup-like liquid at the bottom of the bowl. This is the part you'll drink.

Pour everything from the bowl into a medium jar with a tight lid.

Keep this jar in the fridge and take a couple of spoonfuls of the syrup every few hours.

How to Sing
"Sana, sana, colita de rana"

I know no one will be able to sing "Sana, sana, colita de rana" to you as well as abuela, but having someone sing this to you will bring you comfort when you are feeling ill. Just make sure you show the lyrics to the person so they say it correctly, mi amor, especially if they don't know Spanish.

The lyrics: Sana, sana, colita de rana, si no sana hoy, sanará mañana.

English translation: Heal, heal, frog's little tail, if you don't heal today, you'll heal tomorrow.

How to Do a
Limpia con Huevo

If you don't know how you came down with this cold or sickness, mi amor, I want you to do this bruja ritual, porque you don't need the mal de ojo in your life.

Step 1. Grab a room-temperature egg and pour rubbing alcohol, Florida water, or salt water over the egg to cleanse it.

Step 2. Start from the top of the head and work your way down while saying: "Que este huevo tenga el poder de sacar todo lo malo que me desean, ya sea por envidia, coraje o mala fe." Or set an intention for what you want to be removed from your body. You can do this, mi amor, or you can have someone else do this as well. It doesn't matter.

Step 3. Once you are done, fill a clear cup with cold or room-temperature water (so the egg doesn't cook), crack the egg on the edge of the cup, and let the egg yolk fall into the cup. (Make sure this is a clear cup so you will be able to see the results.)

Step 4. Let the egg sit for 5 to 10 minutes or you can place the cup underneath your bed overnight. The thing you want to avoid doing is touching the cup. Just let it be, mi corazón.

Step 5. Once time is up, you can read the results of what the yolk says or you can just trust that your ancestors gave you protection and banished any evil energy or sickness you had. If you do decide to read the yolk, mi amor, I suggest going on the computer and searching for what it means as there's no one right answer. Just listen to your intuition, mi corazón. You got this.

How to Take Gatorade to Heal a Cold

Again, you have a good head, mi amor. Let's put it to good use here.

HOW TO NOT GET SICK (AGAIN)

Oh, baby, if you are no longer sick—that's wonderful to hear! ¡Amén! Pero you need to be careful, I don't want you to get sick again, so here are some ways you can take care of yourself when abuela is not able to do so. Don't go outside without wearing a sweater (especially if it's below 70 degrees Fahrenheit).

- Wear socks inside the house at all times.
- Don't go outside or go to bed with wet hair unless you want to get sick.
- Wear el mal de ojo bracelet at all times.
- Say salud when someone sneezes so you don't get a cold or an evil spirit.
- Take your vitamins every night. (I take Papaya enzymes, pero talk with your good-looking doctor to find out what you should take, mi amor.)
- Don't stare at a dog while it poops or you will get a stye on your eye. This is self-explanatory, mi amor.

GOING AFTER WHAT YOU WANT

❧

Abuela Rules for Your Money and Career

When it comes to your career, I want you to know that your familia is so proud of everything that you have already accomplished in your life—and you have so many more years ahead of you! I know you are here to hear wise words of wisdom from your abuela, pero you don't need it, mi amor. You are doing so well with your education, you are wise beyond your years, and you are incredibly intelligent. As your abuela, I am so proud of you.

Tu familia is so proud of you. You are going so far. The future looks good for you.

🖤 ABUELA TIP 🖤

Just remember: as long as you do your best, you will get good results.

Pero if you want advice, mi amor, abuela will give you career advice. While I know things are different from when I was a working woman, there are a few things I know I can talk about (I'm not *that* old!).

Career Advice That Will Make You Go Far in Life

∽

FIRST THINGS FIRST...

You Are Never Too Old to Educate Yourself

Whether you are eight or eighty-eight years old, if you are still breathing on this earth, then you can learn something new, baby. Look at your abuela: I became a beautician when I was una jovencita and then I started selling items online to make more money as I got older. I went to school or taught myself how to do these things because life is too short to wait around for others to give you opportunities when they may never come.

This is why it's so important to get an education and a career (whatever that means for you, mi amor) and to continue to study "life" way after la escuela. Just because you finish school doesn't mean you stop learning. If I can learn something new in my old age, then so can you, my smart grandchild.

The hard truth: Most of the time, you have to create the opportunities yourself to show others what you are capable of—but don't let others doubt you or diminish your skills. You are talented, creative, and smart. After all, you are a little mini-me. Keep going after what you want, no matter the cost.

Follow Your Passion

Mi corazón, you are in America, the land of the free and the brave. I know times are different nowadays, pero we came to this country to give our children the freedom to go after what they want; to find a better life. And I won't feel good about the choices I made for mi familia if you are not happy with what you are doing every day of your life. ¿Por qué conformarse? There is no reason to. You deserve happiness above all else, and it's time to reach for the stars and make it happen.

💜 ABUELA TIP 💜
If you are having a hard time figuring out what you are passionate about, take a Sunday as a day of reflection. I know Sunday is supposed to be the day of rest, pero I cannot rest if you do not know what to do with your life or this next chapter. So do this for me, mi corazón.

The hard truth: If you do not enjoy what you're doing or find passion in your job, you are just getting up every day like a robot and living life in a routine that could be draining your hopes and dreams. It's time to figure out what you want to accomplish and want for your-self, mi corazón.

If Something Doesn't Feel Right, then Go in the Opposite Direction

When you are navigating your career, mi amor, you have to listen to your intuition. Punto. No one else knows the right path for you to take besides you, my baby. Yes, your tías might have their opinions on what they believe you should be doing for a living—and I know I even said a few things here and there—pero you are the only person who will be doing this job or career every day of your life, so why listen to others when they have no stake in the matter?

For instance, if you are getting restless at your job because you want to do something more, then figure it out. I say this with love, pero escúchame: no one else can make the change besides you. And if your intuition tells you something isn't right, you need to respect and listen to it.

For you to get anywhere in life, you must have the desire to get there, and I know that you have it within you, mi cielo. You want more out of life and your career because you know that you can do more than you're doing now—and that's what is going to push you to follow your dreams. This is a part of your journey. God has given you the courage to keep going and accept all the things that are in front of you. Don't give up.

The hard truth: Whatever you do, mi amor, don't let others bully you into a situation that doesn't feel right. There are a lot of people out there who will have ulterior motives and will pretend to do things for your "best interests," pero no—we don't have time for people who are not honest with their intentions. If they have to lie and manipulate to get what they want, then we will not give them the time of day. Nunca.

Put Yourself First Above All Else

If there is one thing that you do for your career, it's to put yourself first. I don't mean to be rude to others or ignore requests of your superiors (unless they are full of nonsense, then put them in their place). What I mean is no job is worth your health, relationships, or friendships. Sí, having a career is importante, pero it shouldn't define who you are as a person, as a friend, as a daughter or son, or as a partner. There is simply more to life than just having a job. Remember that, mi amor. There is life to live.

The hard truth: I want you to take care of yourself, mi corazón. Don't overwork yourself. Take weekends off and hang out with your little friends, ¡vayan a bailar! Go live life. Life is too short to do things that are making you unhappy and unhealthy. This is where boundaries come in, and if you don't set boundaries with others, then they will walk all over you—and you are better than that, mi vida.

MONEY SUPERSTITIONS— AHEM, TIPS— TO FOLLOW

Now that you have an adult job—and I say this with love—don't be careless with your dinero. You got an education for a reason, mi amor, and it's time to use that brain of yours to keep your money in the bank. Don't give your money away to your novia o novio or spend it carelessly on things you don't need. Instead, I'm going to give you some money tips you can follow so you can actually retire with money in the bank. (And, claro que sí, some may believe these ideas are superstitions, pero that doesn't mean you shouldn't still follow these rules!)

• **Don't put your bag on the floor.** Ay, por favor, please don't put your purse or any bag on the floor. Not when you're at home, eating out with your little friends, ¡nunca! If you do, you will lose and have bad luck with money. Pero the floor is also dirty, so why ruin a perfectly good bag, mi amor? Think about it.

• **Do not scratch an itchy palm.** If the palm of your hand is itching—don't touch it! It means money is coming your way. Do you have a million dollars in your bank account? That's what I thought; listen to your abuela, por favor.

• **If you wear yellow underwear on New Year's Eve, the new year will bring you money.** Do you want more money, mi amor? Then it's time to buy underwear amarillo, pronto! Put on a fresh pair of underwear first thing in the morning. You don't want to go into the New Year with dirty underwear, do you?

ABUELA'S FAMOUS RECIPES

Ay, mi amor. If I could cook for you all day, I would. Just tell abuela whatever you need, and I'm there. Nada de dieta—you need to eat to be strong! Remember you have an abuela who loves you very much and will always take care of you. But on the off chance that I'm unable to make you your favorite things, I want you to have the below recipes at your disposal so you can cook them yourself whenever you want—because I know that you are a strong, independent person who can make their own meals (but remember, abuela loves to take care of you too).

DESAYUNO
How to Make Farina

I don't know if you remember, mi corazón, but I used to make you farina most mornings when you were little and stayed over at my house. You even used to beg me for it—even though it's considered a healthy breakfast! You can't be eating cornflakes all the time. So if you are ever in the mood to taste abuela's cooking, here's how to make it, my love.

💜 ABUELA PRONUNCIATION 💜
Por favor, it's pronounced "brefas" y "con flay."

....

1⅓ cups milk (you liked it with whole milk,
  pero you can use whatever milk you want)
A pinch of salt
3 tablespoons farina
1 teaspoon white sugar
¼ teaspoon cinnamon

....

Put the milk and the salt in a small pot and let it come to a boil over medium-high heat.

Once the milk is boiling, turn off the heat and slowly sprinkle in the farina until the milk is completely mixed with the cream of wheat.

Once everything is mixed, stir in the sugar.

Pour the farina into a bowl and sprinkle the cinnamon on top (pero you liked it with a lot of cinnamon, mi amor, so go crazy).

How to Make
Papas a la Huancaína
(a Peruvian Recipe)

Every time your friends would come over to visit, they would ask me to make this dish. See, your abuela knows how to cook! But if you ever want to make this yourself, this is how you can do it.

....

3 Peruvian yellow chili peppers or habanero peppers (with seeds and veins removed)

½ pound queso fresco

2 to 4 soda crackers

A little bit of evaporated milk

1 clove of garlic, peeled

Salt to taste

6 to 8 potatoes, rinsed and peeled (yellow Peruvian potatoes or Yukon Gold or young potatoes)

¼ cup vegetable oil

A squeeze of lemon, for serving (optional)

2 to 4 boiled eggs, for garnish

8 leaves of lettuce, for garnish

8 black olives, pitted and halved, for garnish

....

Cut the pepper any way you want, mi amor—but make sure that the seeds and the veins are removed. (You can skip ahead if you prefer to use store-bought aji amarillo paste, mi amor.)

Place the peppers in a medium pot with water and let the water come to a boil over medium-high heat. Don't forget to cover the pot. Once the water comes to a boil, you'll want to cook the peppers for 7 to 10 minutes or until the peppers are completely soft.

Once the peppers are cooked, drain and peel them.

Next, put the peeled peppers (or ½ cup store-bought aji amarillo paste) in a blender along with the queso fresco, crackers, evaporated milk, garlic, and salt.

Blend all the ingredients together until the consistency is smooth. (It shouldn't be chunky, mi amor! Make sure it is all blended well together! This is your Huacaína sauce.)

Don't forget to boil your eggs and potatoes as well! You can boil them together or separately. Just make sure that the potatoes are soft and the egg yolks are fully cooked. (This should take around 12 minutes for the eggs and 15 minutes for the potatoes, depending on their size.)

Meanwhile, spread the lettuce on a serving plate. Once the potatoes and eggs are cooked, cut them in half (make sure to do this after de-shelling the eggs, mi amor) and place them on the plate with lettuce.

Pour the Huancaína sauce all over the potatoes and garnish with the boiled eggs and black olives.

How to Make Arroz con Pollo

(a Puerto Rican Recipe)

I know you love this dish so much because it tastes like home to you, mi amor—but there isn't a lot of measuring when it comes to this dish, it's just made with a lot of love, so the quantities listed below are approximate. Just taste it throughout to see if it tastes like abuela's. Don't worry, mi amor, it will take time to cook like abuela, but you will figure it out before you know it!

2 tablespoons olive oil

1 medium yellow onion, chopped

3 cloves of garlic, minced

2 tablespoons sofrito (homemade is best, but Goya will do)

2 tablespoons recaito (same as above, mi amor)

2½ cups basmati white rice

2 to 3 medium yellow potatoes, chopped

1 tablespoon Goya sazón seasoning

Salt and pepper to taste

2 cups frozen peas or pigeon peas

2 pounds bone-in chicken

In a large pot, drizzle a little bit of olive oil and add the chopped onion and cook for a few minutes over medium-high heat until it begins to look a little see-through.

Add the minced garlic and cook for about a minute (not too much, though, mi amor—you don't want the garlic to overcook).

Next, add the sofrito and the recaito to the pot, stir everything together, and let it simmer for about 5 minutes.

Now add the rice, the chopped potatoes, the peas, the sazón seasoning and salt and pepper, and fill with water over the halfway point of the pot so there's enough room for the rice, peas, and potatoes to cook. Make sure to stir everything together.

Then, add the bone-in chicken directly into the sopa mixture. Cover the pot and let it cook for 30 to 45 minutes or until the rice is nice and fluffy and the potatoes and chicken are fully cooked and tender.

When everything is done, uncover the pot and use a fork to fluff up the rice, and check that the chicken has fully cooked. Once everything looks good, you can plate it up!

Bonus Tip: I like to add avocado slices with a little olive oil on top and serve with a side salad with big slices of tomatoes and Italian dressing. Don't forget your black beans, mi amor. It will really make the dish.

CELEBRATING THE HOLIDAYS

❧

From Christmas to New Year and Birthdays

No matter how old you are, it's important to take the time to celebrate the holidays with your loved ones, mi amor. There are only a few times a year when you can join together with your familia, cook, and dance together. Don't you remember how good it feels to be able to spend time doing what makes us happy with the people we love with all our hearts? Ay, listen to me, baby. You never know when it will be the last time you see tus primos o tías y tíos, so it's importante to let bygones be bygones and show compassion to those you love the most.

It's also important to keep up with the traditions while being able to create your own with your futura familia. For instance, do you remember when I used to make you the cinnamon rice pudding when you were little or when tú y tus primos would yell, "¡Pan, arepa, cafe con leche!" first thing in the morning at mi casa before el desayuno?

Pero if you don't remember which traditions to keep for the holidays, don't worry, mi corazón—here are some ideas you can do moving forward.

New Year's Eve Traditions

∾

1. Eat twelve grapes at midnight. Listen to me, mi ángel. You must eat these twelve grapes within the first twelve seconds of the New Year. This will give you good fortune! Also, make a wish for every grape you eat. It's about being optimistic about what you want to bring into the New Year—so don't forget to make a wish!

2. Wear red underwear for love. If you do this, mi amor, you will finally find that partner you've been searching for on your Plenty of Fish account or whatever dating app you're now on. (Have you tried Christian Mingle yet?) Pero you know it doesn't really matter to me, as long as you find someone who loves you.

3. Clean your house from top to bottom. Do you want to bring those bad, dusty vibras into the New Year? I don't think you want that. Why not take some time to clean your apartment to get all the bad spirits out?

4. Throw a pot of water out the window. If you don't have time to clean your home, mi amor, it's okay—just make sure to throw a pot of water out the balcony or window to get rid of any bad energy you might have in tu casa!

5. Walk around your neighborhood with a suitcase. Ay, mija, mijo, you are always wanting to spend money on traveling, so why not put that good luck out into the world by packing up a suitcase and running around the block to make this a reality? Sí, you may look un poco loco, pero don't mind the neighbors—they will always be chismosos no matter what.

Christmas Traditions

1. El Día de la Inmaculada Concepción. I know you're not that religious anymore and I respect that even though I would love for you to still go to church every now and then—pero if there's one tradition I would love for you to keep up, it's El Día de la Inmaculada Concepción on December 8. ¿Por qué? Porque it celebrates the life of the Virgin Mary.

Pero if you are looking for a less religious reason to celebrate, this is also the beginning of the Christmas season for us Latinos, so this is when you would want to decorate your tree, mi amor.

2. Put a nativity scene (o pesebres y belenes) under the tree. Escúchame, if you don't have a nativity scene already, mi amor, please buy one before the Christmas holiday. It is important for you to have one under your tree for abuela because it celebrates el Niño Jesus and the Three Wise Men. Also, if you want, mi amor, you can hide the little baby Jesus until Christmastime to indicate when he was born.

Or you can celebrate la novena, which is a nine-day celebration leading up to Christmas where you can say a prayer in front of the nativity scene. Either way, mi corazón, buy one before it's too late.

3. Celebrate Christmas on Christmas Eve (otherwise known as Nochebuena). I know a lot of Americans prefer to celebrate on December 25; however, in our culture, we celebrate the anticipation of El Niño Jesus's birthday on the eve of December 24.

I don't know if you remember when you were little, my ángel, pero this is when we would play our favorite Christmas songs, have a big meal with our familia, and open our presents at midnight—and on December 25, we relax.

❤ ABUELA SIDE NOTE ❤

If you don't celebrate Christmas, that's okay, mi corazón. As long as you have faith or a spiritual connection to something larger than yourself, then that's all that matters! Building a relationship with your spiritual beliefs—whether it's with Islam, Judaism, Hinduism, Buddhism, or, ey, astrología (que en paz descanse, Walter Mercado)—will provide you consuelo when you need it most. ¡Claro!

I also have a lot of amigas y amigos who I play dominoes with that practice other religions too! The beauty about our friendships is that we're able to learn from and celebrate with one another every holiday season (¡ay, and year-round también!) Lo que importa is to honor your traditions during the holiday season, religious or not, mi amor.

Holiday and Birthday Cards from Abuela

Mi corazón, do you remember when I used to send you cards for your birthday every year with little dollar bills inside when you were little? I know you are making money with your adult job now, pero I don't want you to forget this little token of love. Here are some of the things I used to write to you every year so you can have them as a memory.

Birthday Card

Hola, mi cielo,

I hope you have a birthday just as amazing as you are. I want you to remember something: Life not only brings you birthdays to celebrate, but it's also a time to reflect on one's life to  see which way you want to go and figure out what truly will make you happy, who you want to take with you on your travels, leave marks that you want to leave in this world, and what impression you make while you are here.

Mira, this is because we are all here for a purpose. Our failures do not follow us for years, they are learning tools for us to grow, mi amor. And when one learns and realizes that, then it's the best birthday gift anyone can have.

Love,
Your abuela

Christmas Card

Feliz Navidad, mi ángel,
May the spirit of this beautiful season bless you always! I wish you with all my heart to enjoy Christmas, in harmony, humbleness, and with the true spirit of Christmas. Wishing that el Niño Jesús brings the peace to accept what cannot change and courage to keep fighting for the things that can. May your gift be happiness and above all, much health!

I love you,
Tú abuela

Three Kings Day Card

Happy Three Kings Day, mi vida,

I'm wishing you many blessings. Remember to visit abuela once in a while. I love and miss you—even a call will suffice! I miss hearing your voice. I got you some socks.

Love,
Abuela

How to Make Coquito
(a Puerto Rican Recipe)

To celebrate el Niño Jesús, let's cheers to His day. I know you love this cocktail, mi amor, so here is your aunt's recipe that she shared with me through the telephone. Make sure you call her to thank her before it's too late.

1 can sweetened condensed milk

1 can evaporated milk

1 can Goya cream of coconut

Vanilla (to taste, pero not too much!)

Cinnamon (to taste, usually a few dashes will do)

Nutmeg (to taste, usually a few dashes will do; don't go crazy)

¾ cup (or more to taste) Don Q rum or Bacardí white rum

Place all ingredients in a blender and mix well.

Put it in a drink container and refrigerate for at least half an hour.

If it gets thick, let it sit at room temperature for a bit, then serve and enjoy.

Bonus Tip: Don't forget to shake well before serving. And garnish with more nutmeg if you want, mi amor.

How to Make Sangría

Oh, so you want to make abuela's sangria? The sangria that all your friends love and rave about? Por supuesto que sí, es deliciosa, like tu abuela. Okay, escucha con mucha atención . . .

1 standard bottle red wine (usually 750 mL)

Fruit medley (typically strawberries and apples)

1 liter bottle Sprite

1 standard bottle orange juice

A splash of Cointreau (optional)

Find a big decanter or jug and fill it up midway with your red wine of choice.

Cut up the fruit into bite-size pieces and put them into the red wine an hour or more to let the fruta soak. (You want the fruta to be drunk with red wine, mi amor.)

Once the fruta has been marinating for a few hours, fill the rest of the container with Sprite and orange juice. Make sure you stir to mix all the flavors together.

Finally, top it off with Cointreau and that's it!

ABUELA SAYINGS WHEN SHE'S HAD TOO MUCH TO DRINK DURING THE HOLIDAYS

- Is there rum in this coquito? I don't taste it. Let's add a little more.

- Ay, mi cielo, I snuck a few more tamales into your takeaway container, pero don't tell your primos.

- I would have been a groupie to Marc Anthony, pero your abuelo wouldn't let me leave.

- Mira, I had a few sips of wine while I was pregnant with your tío—and he turned out fine (for the most part).

- If anything happens to my baby dog, you have to bury his ashes with mine. Don't roll your eyes—he has to be with me for him to go to doggy heaven!

- ¡No me jodas!

- You know, if I were twenty years younger, I would be all over that Bad Bunny.

DEVELOPING RELATIONSHIPS

With Family, Friends, and Other Loved Ones

Ay, mi amor . . . there's nothing like familia. Think about it. Your cousins are your first friends who tell you how to share, laugh, and dance. Your tías and tíos are your first teachers who teach you about the world. Your mamá y papá are your first loves who show you how to connect with others and yourself. And your abuela is your first best friend who will show you what unconditional support looks like no matter what.

But as you get older, these relationships are replaced with new ones. Instead of seeing your familia every day, you'll go to work and be with your coworkers.

Rather than waking up in your childhood home, you'll wake up next to your partner in the home that you built together. All these changes might be scary at first. But remember, you are meant to leave the nest to make a whole new life for yourself. (Pero if you want to live with abuela forever, I would love that. You know you are always welcome here. This is your home, mi amor.)

How to Make Friends That Become Family

∽

When you do leave your home to start your own path, you are going to meet so many new people. Yes, you probably will have your little friends from middle or high school who used to come over to mi or your parents' casa to hang out—by the way, how are they doing? Is so-and-so still seeing that one person? Oh, they broke up? That's a shame—but it's a different ball game when you finish high school because everyone is at the stage where they're trying to figure themselves out, experience new hormones, and grow up all at the same time.

While meeting new people and having new experiences will be an exciting time, you have to remember that who you choose to surround yourself with will impact not only how you view yourself but also how you choose to connect with others around you. *Dime con quién andas, y te diré quién eres.*

People don't talk about this enough, pero tus amigos y amigas are some of the most important relationships you will ever have in your life. Punto. There's no obligation to be with them—unlike family—yet you choose to connect with them. Since these are one of the few relationships that are based on choice, you want to make sure you are making the right ones because the last thing I want for you, mi sol, is for you to hang out with the wrong crowd. You are my little innocent angel who shouldn't be coerced, or I will find them and hit them with my chancla.

So how do you know when you've found the right friends who will become tu familia? Don't worry, abuela is going to tell you.

How to Know You Found the Right Friends

൦

THEY ASK YOU QUESTIONS ABOUT YOURSELF.

When you first begin to hang out with new people, you may be eager to make a connection—pero don't lose sight of yourself, mi amor. While it might be exciting to make a new friend or two, you want to make sure that they are not selfish and only talk about themselves.

💔 ABUELA TIP 💔

For example, when I talk to your friends or meet new people, I try to ask them questions to get to know them better, especially if I haven't seen them in a long time. I don't make the whole conversation about me—and you shouldn't either, mi amor.

The thing you want to be aware of is how the talk is flowing between the both of you: Are they only talking about themselves? Do you feel like you're being listened to? Are they constantly interrupting you without apologizing or acknowledging their interruptions in some way? Are they on their teléfono while you're talking? Eso es maleducado.

Even though these new friends might have the best intentions, it's importante for you to listen to your intuition, mi corazón—and if you feel like something is off within the first conversation or two, then it's time to listen to your gut and walk away.

THEY DON'T MAKE YOU QUESTION YOUR VALUES OR INTENTIONS, OR HAVE YOU SECOND-GUESS YOURSELF.

Ay, mija, mijo, no friendship is worth losing yourself over. ¿Me entiendes? You are too important to change yourself so someone will like you more. Pero ¿por qué? Remember God made you perfect just the way you are, so why would you need to change yourself?

I don't know if you already know this, pero a good friend will make it a point to understand your values, your beliefs, and your independence. They should never make you do something you don't feel comfortable doing. They should never force you to change your mind when they have ill intentions behind these actions. Sí, it's importante to have conversations about important topics to better understand something or someone, like politics, race, history, even religion—pero they must also respect you. Punto. No relationship can ever grow out of disrespect; and that's a fact. *Mejor solo que mal acompañado*.

THEY DON'T PUT UP WITH YOUR MIERDA.

Te amo, mi amor, pero you need friends who won't put up with your attitude. We all have our demons—including your abuela—pero a true friend shouldn't stand by you and let you make big mistake after big mistake that could ruin your life because they are afraid to "ruin the friendship" or say something that is "going to hurt you." ¡Olvídate de eso!

A good friend isn't afraid to tell you the hard truth—in a tactful way, claro que sí. If they believe you are in a toxic relationship, they should talk to you about it. If they are worried about your health because you started to pick up smoking or drinking a lot more, they need to call you, rápido! Good friends will know you best—outside of your familia and significant other, of course—so if they don't respect you enough to tell you the truth, then they don't deserve your friendship.

No lie is worth telling just to keep the peace.

THEY MAKE YOU LAUGH.

I knew I found my friends for life when they made me laugh so hard that I almost peed my pants—don't laugh, it's true! Your best friends need to make you want to pee your pants every once in a while, mi amor—if not, then life isn't worth living!

Mira, I'm not saying that they have to be a comedian like Charo—or what is that other guy's name? Jerry Seinfeld?—But they shouldn't take life too seriously, mi amor. Life is already tough enough, so find friends who will make you forget the world's troubles every now and then.

THEY WILL SUPPORT YOU THROUGH THICK AND THIN.

Even though a good friend should never put up with your antics, mi amor, a true friend will give it to you straight while still being supportive. Pero listen, there is a thin line here. For instance, if you are being dis-respectful, they should not feel obligated to stay in a friendship that is no longer built out of respect and trust. (I know that is hard to hear, mi corazón, but it's true. No one should be obligated to put up with abuse—no one.)

Pero a friendship can never blossom into a beautiful flower if someone is always leaving when things get tough. If that is the case, they don't really care about your well-being, mi corazón.

💜 ABUELA REMINDER 💜

Una mesa no puede volverse estable sin apoyo.

You want someone in your life who is going to call or text you in the morning to see how you're doing after telling them about a breakup or divorce.

You want a friend who will help you move.

You want someone to listen to your worries or concerns if you're going through a rough time.

If your friends make up excuses for not being able to help or support you in some way or another over and over again, then cut them out of your life. It's better to be alone than to deal with imposters, my love. *And once you throw out the trash, you don't bring it back in.*

How to Prepare for Parenthood
❧

If you ever become a parent one day (no pressure, mi amor, pero, just so you know, I would love to hold my great-grandchildren before I go to Heaven), I want you to understand the kind of responsibility you will have. Sí, it will be the most rewarding experience you will ever have, pero it will also be one of the hardest things you will ever do in your life.

I may make it look easy (after all, I have been on this earth for quite some time and know what I'm talking about), pero I had to learn just like you will one day—and remember, I didn't have the "internet" like the kids have today. Sí, I am, cómo se dice, "tooting my own horn."

💜 ABUELA PRONUNCIATION 💜
Ay, I said internet because I know you always laugh when I say "weefee," pero that's the only way I know how to say it!

So until that day comes, I am going to share with you everything you will need to know to best prepare for parenthood. So grab a cafecito, mi amor, you are going to need it.

HOW TO BECOME THE KIND OF PARENT YOU ARE PROUD TO BE

This will not happen overnight—and you may even second-guess yourself, but don't beat yourself up, mi vida; no parent knows what they're doing when a newborn enters their life, even if they read all the books and receive all the advice. No one will know how they will handle the day-to-day until that baby is in their arms. Punto.

Before then, I want you to take care of yourself, tu partner y tu casa. Do whatever you need to do to have things ready for when the bebé comes, because once that bebé comes, that's all that will matter. And if you are beginning to panic, don't worry, tu familia will be there every step of the way.

🖤 ABUELA ADVICE FOR NIETOS 🖤

Remember this, mijo: You are the man in her life. And you are her support structure. You're going to need to support her when she needs it. You must always be there for her from this point on. You have to do what needs to get done to make sure you both are on a healthy and happy path; not just for you two, pero also for the bebé. Just make sure you're there to support her every step of the way. She comes first, not you.

HOW TO PREPARE FOR BEBÉ

- **Set up the baby room with everything you need and babyproof tu casa.** Tu familia can help you with this. Tus tías o primos still have a lot of bebé stuff they can pass down. Just take it, mi amor, that's what familia is for.

- **Make sure to go to every doctor's visit.** Do I need to say more? And don't forget to tell tu familia about your appointments, so they can go with you.

- **Visit tu familia often.** Listen, this is an abuela requirement: we need to make sure you and your partner are taking care of yourselves—and a phone call will not do. I need to look into your eyes to make sure you're okay.

- **¡Monja!** You and your partner need to stay full! Come to abuela's and I'll make sure to cook you both something delicious.

- **Get romántico con tu husband or wife.** Ay, do you only want to be lying on the couch and eating finger foods for nine months straight or while you wait for the adoption to clear? No. You're an adult and you need to still have coochie-coochie time. ¡Es importante!

💜 ABUELA SAYS 💜

Ay, what is this I hear about a babymoon? ¿Qué es eso? A vacation before your baby comes? Ay, Dios mío—what is up with kids nowadays? You don't have time for a baby-moon. Where are you going to go, Kansas? The Bahamas? No. If you want to go on vacation, come to abuela's, and I'll take care of you. I'll call it Hotel de la Abuela. I'll make you sopa, rub your feet, and sing "Sana, sana, colita de rana." Don't spend money if you don't have to, you need to save that for the bebé.

WHAT TO DO WHEN THE BEBÉ ARRIVES

Okay, mi cielo, quiero que me escuches con atención: your life is going to change dramáticamente. I don't want to scare you, pero it's importante to be honest, so you fully understand what to expect.

When I had tu mamá, I knew that I was ready to become a mamá myself, pero I wasn't expecting how tired I was going to feel or how my body was going to change—pero that is life, and we have to make do with what God gives us.

♥ ABUELA QUOTES ♥

"Lord, grant me the strength to accept the things I cannot change, the courage to change the things I can, and the wisdom to know the difference."

Para ti, mi vida, you are going to be okay. It's natural for these changes to happen, but instead of worrying about trying to be a perfect parent, it's more importante to just make sure that the ship is running smoothly. Everyone will have their part to play—including the bebé—so just take one day at a time. As long as everyone is eating, sleeping, and has support, then everything will work out in the end.

🩶 ABUELA ADVICE: 🩶
THE BEBÉ IS HERE, NOW WHAT?

• **Get the baby's birth certificate ahora.** Just in case anything happens, it's important to get this as soon as possible, my love. Hide it in a good spot.

• **Take a shower.** Again, I say this with love, pero if you don't shower once in a while, the baby is going to think their parents are stinky—and that bebé already lives in their own toilet.

• **Visit tu familia**. Ay, if you don't visit tu familia, don't get mad if we show up at your door. I need to see my great-grandchild (and you, of course, mi amor).

• **Get some rest.** You both just went through a lot of changes in a short amount of time, so, por favor, let tu familia help you—don't fight it. I know you think you're independent and can do this on your own, pero tu mamá already said she was going to be staying at your house the minute the child comes, so just make your mother happy, por favor, so you can get some rest.

When to Use the Chancla

When your children become teenagers, they will become ruthless, like little mocosos. Tu mamá was the same, even if she believes differently, así que no le hagas caso. When the time comes, I want you to understand why the chancla can be an important tool for discipline and when you should use it. Perdóname, mi vida, I know your generation doesn't like this form of punishment, pero es importante. And, mira, let me tell you a secret, you don't actually use it. Just flash it every once in a while to get the message across— watch, they will get in line.

¿Por qué usar la chancla? ¿Por qué no? Next question, ¡carajo!

¿CUÁNDO USAR LA CHANCLA?

- They disrespect you.

- They don't listen to you.

- They don't respond when you call for them.

- They bring their novio o novia into the house when you're not around.

- They cheat while playing games, like Monopoly or Lotería.

FALLING AND STAYING IN LOVE WITH YOUR SPOUSE

Ay, qué lindo! You want some wisdom about relationships from your abuela—well, you came to the right place, mi bebé. First of all, I have a few questions para ti . . .

- Are they a person of God?

- Do they make enough money to take care of you and themselves?

- Do they want to have children? (¡Porque sabes que quiero bisnietos!)

Now that we got that out of the way, I want you to remember one thing (and I know you're not going to like what I'm about to say, pero escúchame): No relationship will ever work if you don't love (or at least try to understand) yourself first. ¿Me entiendes? I'm not saying you have to be perfect (even though you are perfect in God's eyes and mine), pero before you dive into a relationship with someone, first and foremost, you have to be respectful of yourself. If you don't respect yourself, others will notice and stop respecting you—because if this is how you treat yourself, then you're showing others that it's okay for them to treat you the same way.

The fact of the matter is respect is the foundation of all healthy relationships, so do me a favor, mi amor, stop letting others walk all over you and learn to love and respect yourself now and always. You are not a road to be walked on.

Mira, how about this: Before you even begin dating and smooching other people, why not date yourself first? ¡Qué buena idea! If you get to know yourself first, you'll know what kind of requirements to set, how you want to be treated, what kind of partner you're looking for, and so on. I'm going to share some ways you can show up for yourself first before getting into a committed relationship.

Abuela's Acts of Self-Love

ॐ

LEARN TO BE INDEPENDENT

Get your education, find a good job, and save your din-ero ahora, so you don't have to depend on anybody, because if you're ever unhappy with a person, you won't have to continue to be with them since you'll have mucho dinero in the bank and a degree in your back pocket.

The last thing you ever want to feel is stuck in a relationship. So many people are forced to stay with people they no longer want to create and share a life with because they're financially unable to leave, and I don't want that for you, mi cielo. You deserve to be happy no matter the circumstance—this is why you need to build a good foundation for yourself from the ground up.

TAKE CARE OF YOUR HEALTH

I know a lot of familias don't believe in therapy, pero I'm hip with the times and I believe doing this will be good for you. Your relationship with your mind and body is one of the most important relationships you will ever have—and just like any other partnership, it's importante for you to nurture, support, and show up for yourself so you can build a strong foundation of mental and physical strength.

💪 ABUELA TIP 💪

I want you to think of taking care of yourself like a tree growing more roots into the ground, my baby. The more you do this, the more stable and grounded you'll feel when a storm comes.

Look, as long as you are finding ways to take care of your health however you see fit, then that works, mi corazón. This is something I wish I did when I was a young mujer, so that's why I'm telling you this now.

It might feel like a lot of work (and it will be), pero having a strong mind is critical to navigating life's challenges. Others will try to trick you or ignore your needs, and I want you to be able to take care of yourself. The truth is, even though tus amigos y familia can come to your rescue or provide support, it's also important for you to show up for yourself just like how you would for a friend or family member. You got this, mi chiqui.

BUILD A STRONG COMMUNITY

I know it might sound a little opposite to what I said earlier about being independent, but escúchame, you can be your own best friend and still have support and love from others. Just because you know how to be alone doesn't mean you should be alone—because you have a life to live and it's better to be shared with others.

The reason why you want to build a community before you get into a relationship is because your social circle affects your whole life, mi corazón, and if you don't have a support system to begin with, then your partner will become your whole life, and that's not healthy.

You need friends, coworkers, familia, and even mentors to share life experiences with. You don't have to do *everything* with your partner, no matter how handsome or beautiful they may look. Even I do things on my own without your abuelo. I still play board games with my little friends. It's about balance (and he misses me when I leave).

Just remember to still put in the effort with people in your social circle long after you're in a relationship. Just because you got a new plant doesn't mean you should stop watering the old ones.

How to Know That You Found the Right Person

‿❧

Ay, so you think you found the one? And you think this person has what it takes to take care of mi ángel? ¡Qué bueno! (Of course, no one can take care of you as well as your abuela.) Pero just because you believe this person is tu alma gemela, it's still importante to go through abuela's amor checklist to absolutely make sure this will be the person you will marry under the eyes of God. (You will be getting married in a church, right?)

ABUELA AMOR CHECKLIST

- Do they give you their jacket or a blanket when you're cold?

- Do they make you a cafecito in the mañana when you first wake up?

- Do they bring flores to your mama or familia every time they visit?

- Do they communicate their love to you in emotional and physical ways?

- Do they respect you, or how you say: "Your boundaries, your body, your time?" (See, I listen to you, baby.)

- Do they make you laugh?

- Do they enjoy your company and do you enjoy theirs?

Of course, this is not everything to consider, pero what's most importante is how you are as a team. A partnership is not a one-way road, it's a two-way street, and as long as you both keep the doors open to communication, everything is going to work out in the end, te lo prometo.

It's also important to note that no one can tell you what or how your relationship should or shouldn't look like—that is completely up to you and your partner. While you should never accept abuse in any shape or form, there are no rules on how to thrive in a relationship. What works for you and your partner might not work for another couple and that is completely okay. At the end of the day, there needs to be trust between the both of you so that you have each other's back no matter what.

❤ **ABUELA TIP** ❤

Love has no judgment, only encouragement.

IF THE RELATIONSHIP IS IN A RUT

Pero even though you know all of this, mi amor, it's still important for you and your significant other to keep the spark alive—ay, so many of your tías lost their partners because they simply thought love was supposed to be easy to maintain. ¿Sabes lo que es eso? Pereza. Love is not easy; it's hard work, and you have to put in the effort to receive the sweet reward. That means you can't run away when things get tough, porque there will always be battles to go through.

And if your partner is not working as hard as you on the relationship and they're not adding any value to your life, then it's time to kick them to the curb because the relationship is just shit and it's not worth shit. (Again, pardon my language. Some things have to be said.)

💜 ABUELA TIP 💜

Maybe if you kids stop looking at your phones all the time, you could actually connect with the people you are in a relationship with. It's importante to look into each other's eyes and remember why you fell in love with one another in the first place—so promise me you will put your phone away, mi amor.

However, if the both of you are putting in the effort, but there is still a lull happening in the relationship, then you have to put the romance back into the relationship! ¡Claro que sí! Your grandpa snores in our bed every single night, but we still give each other kisses in the morning, even though I want to smother him with my pillow sometimes. So here are some date night ideas the both of you can do together.

ROMANTIC DATE NIGHT IDEAS

- **Play dominoes o Lotería and eat ice cream. (You should buy Heavenly Hash en Publix. Es mi preferido.)**

💜 **ABUELA PRONUNCIATION** 💜

It's "Pooblis"! Also, ¿puedes traerme un helado? Gracias, mi amor.

- **Go out dancing!**
- **Cook and dance together in the kitchen with your favorite songs.**

💜 ABUELA MIXTAPE: 💜
LOVE SONGS I RECOMMEND

- "Bésame mucho" by Luis Miguel

- "Vivir mi vida" by Marc Anthony

- "Espérame en el cielo" by Los Panchos

- "Toda una vida" by Antonio Machín

- "Suavecito" by Malo

- **Netflix and chill (Don't "¡Ay, abuela!" me! I am a woman who also has needs.)**

💜 ABUELA PRONUNCIATION 💜

It's pronounced "Neflis." I know this.

WHAT TO DO IF THEY CHEAT

Listen, mi amor, I know that your heart is broken right now, but I want you to listen to me very carefully: no person is worth crying over now when they decided to end the relationship before talking with you. This isn't about love or lust, mi angel, it's about ego and lack of communication porque instead of them talking to you about how unhappy they were or how they needed to end things, they made this choice about the relationship without involving you, and that is not right.

The truth of the matter is that this relationship is over. Punto. Whether you decide to stay with them or not (that is your choice, pero remember, first and foremost, you have to respect yourself), the relationship is dead and you either have to start anew with them or with yourself.

You already know that my opinion is to end things completely and wipe your hands clean, porque no one is going to hurt my baby like that; however, I know this generation views things a little differently, so I want you to know that I will support you in whatever decision you make. Pero I want you to remember one thing: whatever you do, don't pity yourself. You are too strong and have gone through too much already to cry over milk that has already gone bad. De esto saldrá algo mejor. Trust me.

WEATHERING THE STORM

What to Do During Hard Times

T he apple of my eye, I wish I could prevent you from getting hurt; unfortunately, I'm unable to protect you from all the harm the world can sometimes offer. Don't worry, mi amor, you have already proven that you can overcome anything that is thrown your way. You're strong, emotionally intelligent, and resilient. (Of course you are—after all, you're just like me.)

All jokes aside, mi amor, when the world tries to push you down, remember what I told you when you were little: The world is tough, the world is unpredictable. You may never know what will happen, but all you can control is what happens next.

Life will throw you a lot of hurdles for you to overcome—but even though I'm unable to protect you from every little thing, I can provide some words of wisdom for those difficult times you may not fully know how to tackle (even though I know you have the strength within you to do so, my little firecracker).

If You Feel Like You've Failed

∽

The truth is, mi corazón, you have two choices in this world: you could either be a sad dog in the corner or you can get up and recognize that this failure isn't going to change you for the worst. So you have to make a decision that allows you to keep moving forward no matter what—porque remember: it's human to be sad, but it's also human to be resilient.

Of course, it's important to recognize and sit with your feelings to accept what happened, pero only take the day, mi amor, because the more time you lie on the couch, scroll on your "ticky-tacky," and feel sorry for yourself, the less time and energy you'll have to pick yourself up and try again.

I want you to remember something: there is no such thing as failure. Every failure in life teaches you something new either about yourself, your needs, or the situation that you were in. It's time to reflect and figure out what this failure is trying to teach you. Trust me, there's always a lesson.

If People Are Making Fun of You, Talking Behind Your Back, or Simply Not Being Kind

∾

¡No importa! The fact of the matter is people are going to be mean to you, whether it's at school, at your job, or even among your friends and family, but that says more about them than it does about you, mi amor. It's a shame that people are rude, inconsiderate, and mean (ser maleducado no tiene excusas), but at the end of the day, the people who are catty, unfriendly, and malicious do not deserve a seat at the table of your life.

The next time someone is rude to you, I need you to take a step back and ask yourself these questions:

Should you actually be sad about anything right now? Mira, these people are showing you their true colors—if anything, they are doing you a favor so you don't have to deal with them again.

Can you ignore them? Especialmente if you'll never see them again? *Si no tienes nada bueno que decir, mejor no digas nada.*

Can you tell them how they hurt you? They need to hear it, mi amor, so they never do it again. How do you expect people to respect you if they don't know how you want to be treated?

And if you did tell them, mi corazón, did they listen and apologize or did they make up excuses like the pendejos that they are? ¡Ay, cabrones!

The way you answer these questions will determine if you want these relationships in your life anymore—but remember: actions speak louder than words. Don't make excuses for people when they've already shown you who they are. We have to accept what they show us from the start—and not how we wish them to be.

If You're Not Sure About Which Decision to Make

∞

Ay, what are you worried about? That you'll make the wrong decision? So? There is no such thing as a wrong decision, sweetheart. Any decision you make in your life will lead you right to where you need to be and teach you the kinds of lessons you are meant to learn. Además, most decisions in life are never truly permanent. Would your abuela ever lie to you? If you realize that the decision you made wasn't the right move, then change it! ¡Nada es permanente!

💜 **ABUELA TIP** 💜

Started a new job and don't like it? Find another! Cut your hair way too short? Wear a hat and let it grow! Moved across the country to start a new life and it's not making you happy? Move in with me—I'll take care of you. ¡No me importa!

Before you make any decisions, though, you need to listen to what your gut is trying to tell you or pray about it porque God will give you the answers you seek, mi amor. ¡Asegúrate de escuchar! Sometimes the answers are quick and if you are playing your little video games or distracting yourself with the "ticky-tacky," you won't hear them.

Mira, whatever you decide to do at this moment, it's much more importante to live your life with purpose and to make sure you are not compromising your values. If you feel unsure about a situation, don't let a niño o niña tell you how it's "no, big deal." Ay, don't even let your primos o primas try to bully you into making a decision that you are not ready to make. You have to realize that you must take full responsibility for who you are and who you will become after you make these decisions porque no one else can do this for you. So as long as you are making the choice that you are happy with then everything will work out.

If You're Going Through a Breakup or Divorce

Lo siento, mi amor. Heartbreak is never an easy thing to navigate. It doesn't matter if you broke up with them or they broke up with you, either way, the end of a relationship can bring a lot of discomfort and change—and if you don't have the right support, the water can become choppier to sail.

Just know that a breakup does not define you and your worth, mi cielo. Sometimes things just don't work out, and that's okay! You don't want to try to play with a toy that is too broken to fix, right?

🖤 ABUELA THROWBACK 🖤

Ay, when I was younger, boys used to flock to me like a moth to a flame—and could you blame them? You know, most people don't believe I look my age. But no matter how often they tried to get this coochie-coochie (What? Somos todos adultos), I told them I was a woman of God. Aun así lo intentaron.

What I'm trying to say, mi chiqui, is that you cannot force a love that is no longer burning. And if you or your significant other have declared their feelings, it's time to snuff out the flame for now. A partnership should never be dependent on codependency or force. It's about two whole people coming together to build a life together—and if that chapter has ended, it's best to respect your or the other person's needs without trying to change their mind. If the relationship is meant to be, it will work out again, mi vida. And sometimes, it won't make sense. *Pero no le busques la quinta pata al gato.*

If Someone You Love Has Passed Away

Ay, mi corazón. I wish I could take this pain away from you porque I know there is nothing like it, pero I want you to know that you are not alone in feeling what you are feeling. God may have decided it was time for this person to leave this world, but I want you to know that they will always be with you. Siempre.

I know this is easier said than done. This pain will always be with you and you will wish things ended differently for them to still be here, pero escúchame, I want you to try to remember that their legacy will live on in everything that you do, mi amor. And when you have children and tell them about them, their story will live on through them.

Even though they are no longer here doesn't mean they are forgotten, because you will always make sure to keep that flame burning. Te quiero mucho, mi amor. Abuela is here if you need anything.

If Life Just Feels Hard Right Now

∾

As much as we want our lives to run smoothly, unfortunately, life doesn't quite work that way, mi amor. But I want you to remember one thing: without the lows, you won't be able to appreciate the highs. Without the rain, you won't be able to appreciate the sunshine. ¿Me entiendes? This thing we call life is going to have its peaks and valleys—and we cannot control this as much as we want to. But rather than trying to fight the storm, it's more important to make sure your boat is stable and safe enough to weather it. (I am talking about your mind, my love.)

The next time you are feeling lost, sad, or lonely, I want you to say the following phrases to yourself in the mirror.

WORD OF WISDOM TO SAY IN FRONT OF THE MIRROR WHEN LIFE FEELS HARD

- "Life may be hard right now, but this is just temporary."

- "My abuela loves me and that's all that matters." (Did I make you laugh? You know it's true, mi amor.)

- "Algo es algo; menos es nada."

- "As long as I'm laughing, things can never look that bad."

- "Sometimes I cannot let fear stand in the way of my integrity and what I believe in. I have to let my voice be heard."

- "Feeling sorry for myself is the biggest waste of time. I deserve happiness. I deserve stability. And I can give myself these things to feel loved."

- "If someone hurts me, I'll just rub a little dirt on it and I'll be good."

- "I want you to know that I'm very proud of you, and I love you with all my heart."

The truth is, life is what you make of it, mi cora-zón. If you want to be happy, then do what makes you happy. Remember, mi amor, each day you are here on this earth is a gift. So enjoy the happy moments but appreciate the bad ones too. Como te dije antes, there is a lesson in everything we do, and how you choose to respond is more importante than what has happened to us; it is in our control. Take one step at a time and remember that everything will work out. Te lo prometo.

A GOODBYE LETTER FROM ABUELA

Mi corazón,

I'm so glad we had this time together—you know you are the center of my life. I hope my wisdom has given you everything you are looking for. I know that you are going to go far in life—and I am so very proud of you. Never forget how much abuela loves you. My heart is with you always. Just remember to do your best, to be kind to others, and to call tu familia every now and then.

If there is one last piece of wisdom I can give to you, mi cielito, it is to go after what you want with enthusiasm and to make the most out of every moment. Life is too short to be scared of the unknown because we never know what tomorrow will bring. Como dijo Celia Cruz, "¡La vida es un carnaval!"

Now, it's time for sweet dreams and hopes for a better tomorrow. I'm going to have my glass of milk and my chocolate cookies, watch my novelas, and go to bed.

Remember: I love you, I love you more, I love you always, I love you forever. Que Dios te proteja y te bendiga.

Con mucho amor, siempre,
Tu abuela